This book belongs to

_____

_____

Christine Thompson-Wells
Author, Qualified Professional, Accredited Educator &
Independent Writer
BA Education, Dip of Teaching, MACEA

We support Diabetes Type One & Motor Neuron Disease. 10% of the net sales
will be divided equally between both charities.

Our Mission:

Every child and adult have value and is important to us; therefore, we strive through research, online education, and book publishing, to bring life-skill education to all children and all families.

For Education Packages

Please see our book website: www.how2books.com.au and Education packages, www.fullpotentialtraining.com.au
or Contact:
admin@fullpotentialtraining.com.au

Changing lives through knowledge

HORMONES WITH HATS

MEETING CURRICULUM OBJECTIVES – UNITED KINGDOM (UK)

Natural body changes for girls between School Years 4 to 6, ages 9 to 11 years.

(Health and Wellbeing, Relationships, and Living in the Wider World)

Relationships Education, Relationships and Sex Education (RSE) and Health Education.

'Effective RSE does not encourage early sexual experimentation. It should teach young people to understand human sexuality and to respect themselves and others. It enables young people to mature, build their confidence and self-esteem and understand the reasons for delaying sexual activity. Effective RSE also supports people, throughout life, to develop safe, fulfilling, and healthy sexual relationships, at the appropriate time.'[1]

CURRICULUM OBJECTIVES – AUSTRALIA

Incorporating and supporting Years 4-6, ages 9-11 years. Personal, Social and Community Health (ACPPS070 – ACPS076 - ACPPS071 - ACPPS072 - ACPPS073 – and other related areas of the Curriculum including: TLF-IDM021182 Scootle.edu.au).

For School and Family packages, please see Pages 71-72 for further information.

If you have purchased this book without its cover, it may be a stolen book.

---

[1] Relationships and Sex Education (RSE) (Secondary) - GOV.UK (www.gov.uk) Extracted from 'statutory guidance Relationships Education, Relationships and Sex Education (RSE) and Health Education & Australia: https://www.scootle.edu.au

Neither the publisher or the author is under any obligation to provide professional services in anyway, legal, health or in any form which is related to this book, its contents advice or otherwise.

The law and practices vary from country to country and state to state.

If legal or professional information is required, the purchaser, or the reader should seek the information privately and best suited to their particular needs, and circumstances.

This is not a medical book. It is a book developed by the publisher to open the conversation about how the human body changes when growing up.

The author and publisher specifically disclaim any liability that may be incurred from the information within this book.
All rights reserved. No part of this book, including the interior design, images, cover design, diagrams, or any intellectual property (IP), icons and photographs may be reproduced or transmitted in any form by any means (electronic, photocopying, recording or otherwise) without the prior permission of the publisher. ©

Copyright© 2022 MSI Australia

All rights reserved

ISBN: 978-0-6450890-2-8

Published by How2Books
Under licence from MSI Ltd, Australia
Company Registration No: 96963518255
NSW, Australia

See our website: www.how2books.com.au
Or contact by email: sales@how2books.com.au
Covers and Copyright owned by MSI, Australia

MSI acknowledges the author and images, text and photographs used in this book

Children's books

Will Jones Space Adventures & The Money Formula – Book
Will Jones Space Adventures & The Money Formula – The Play
Will Jones & The Money Formula – Educator's Resource Pack
Will Jones Space Adventures & the Zadrilian Queen – Book
Will Jones Space Adventures & The Zadrilian Queen – Play
Will Jones Space Adventures & The Zadrilian Queen – Educator's Resource Pack
There are many more Will Jones Books To Come Out
Dora Damper Makes Honey Damper Bread
Potato Pete Goes to Market
Changes Facing Rosie
Changes Facing Kian
Changes Facing Jai
Changes Facing Caitlin

Books For Adults

Devils In Our Food
Recipes Without Devil Additives
How To Reduce Stress – Find Your Positive Head Space
Making Cash Flow
Selling Made Easy
Know Your Destination 'Go' Learn To Drive Your Mind
The Golden Book Of Whispering Poems and many more books
The Magic of Chelsea
Please see our website

Disclaimer

This is not a medical book and should not be used as such. The contents have been developed through observational theory and research (observational psychology). Information is also drawn from scientific literature and peer-reviewed papers, web search and personal enquiry.

The diagrams are for information and to enhance the meaning of the written text. Statements, information, and ideas within this book are for education purposes only. The text presented allows the reader to draw their own conclusions on the content offered.

Always consult with your doctor for possible illness or underlying illness. Christine Thompson-Wells (MSI) Australia, How2Books.com.au and Full Potential Training.com.au, cannot be held liable for any errors or omissions.

PREFACE

The characters and story within this book are fictitious. If a similar name or identity is drawn from within the writing, it is purely coincidental. The stories are not representative of any one or more individuals. The stories come together through my own unique and individual teaching and life experiences that are brought together to create this book.

Because all children worldwide go through similar bodily changes at similar times growing up, the stories connect with different children worldwide. The places where children are living are used to ground the story. The locations are destinations I have visited on my own life journey.

Each book targets different age and growth spans, and the story base incorporates children's stories, considering, some artistic thought, and writing.

The four books (two for boys and two for girls) are within the series: 'Changes', Children Growing Up, have been designed in a narrative form, (story telling) to assist children and to allow them to naturally adapt to their environment while they go through the different child to adult stages.

It is with sensitivity, that I acknowledge different cultures and traditions, this, and to my best ability, is understood in the writing, illustrations, and storytelling.

HOW TO USE THIS BOOK

In a NEW and exciting approach, hormone characters help our children learn about how their body changes when growing up.

The chapters are the story book. This approach allows the young person to come to grips with how their body and the way they think is changing.

Part two introduces the adults to the story and the information the young person has learnt.

Part three allows both the young adult and older adults to work through the pages together. This process helps the family to celebrate the changes that all young people go through as they go into adulthood.

We encourage both boys and girls to read the four books as they go through their own life changes.

Christine

Contents   Page

PREFACE
How To Use This Book

INTRODUCTION

Chapter One	1
Taking One Step At A Time	
Chapter Two	6
Time Moves On	
Chapter Three	12
The Bologna Book Fair	
Chapter Four	17
Friends Find A Common Interest	
Chapter Five	22
Finding Hormones	
Chapter Six	34
Summer Holidays	
Part Two	
Working Together For Kids And Adults	36
Parents' And Kids' Worksheets	37
Part Three	
Working Together For Kids And Adults	41
Let's Move On	42
Your Girl Child	44
Hormones, How? and Why?	53
A Girl's Progression Stages	56
How Kids Learn	58

Establishing Healthy Habits	61
Your Girl and Her Brain	64
Active Hormones, Personal Hygiene, Wellbeing And Puberty	65
Role Models and Mentors	69
Understanding How The Human Body Grows and Matures & Relationships	70
Online School Packages	71
Family Packages	72

INTRODUCTION

This is the first book in the series of two books for girls. 'Changes' Facing Rosie is a story about a nine-year-old girl who lives in Bologna, Italy. She lives with her family; and has two older sisters and one older brother. Her mum is a graphic designer, her dad works in publishing, both work in Bologna but her mum spends a lot of time working from home.

One of her sisters has trained to be a nurse and is now back at the university where she is training to be a doctor. Her other sister is a hairdresser. Rosie's, brother Ricardo, is seven years older than her and attends the Upper Secondary School, Bologna and is studying science.

She goes to a Lower Secondary School and has two friends that she is close to. Maria is the friend she usually catches the school bus with, and her other friend Isabella is a friend that she likes to spend time with. Both of her friends are different, and each contributes their uniqueness to Rosie's story.

Woven into the story is the visit to one of Bologna's Book Fairs and there starts the interest Rosie has with the subject of biology.

At school, Rosie and Isabella normally play up during Mr Conti's class on biology, but since the girls visit to the book fair, Rosie's interest in the subject has grown deeper. Her interest is further enhanced by her sister's studies of becoming a doctor.

Chapter One
Taking One Step At A Time

The summers of Bologna, Italy, can be hot and dry. Rosie lives in Bologna, she has two older sisters and one older brother, a mum and dad and not to mention Oscar the dog, and Felix the cat.

Rosie is age nine and goes to an English-speaking school in Bologna.

In Italy Secondary School lasts eight years and is comprised of Lower Secondary School, (Scuola secondaria di primo grado) and Upper Secondary School (Scuola secondaria di secondo grado). She loves her school but lately she had felt different. For some reason, she had become much more thoughtful. She somehow knew she was changing and was now taking her schoolwork seriously, whereas, before she would play up in class and get into trouble, but now, she wanted to learn her lessons. She didn't know why she felt this way, but she did. Rosie's school day started at eight and finished by about one-thirty in the afternoon.

It was in the middle of the day, about one-thirty and a hot summer's day in early June and Rosie wanted to finish her essay before she left the classroom. She had explained to her friends, *'I will catch you up at the bus stop, I just want to finish this essay...!'*

The Mistress, Miss Rossi, had given Rosie permission to finish her essay, but to be no longer than ten minutes after the class had finished or 'she could finish it tomorrow!'

Her friend Maria, said, *'Cummon Rosie, the Mistress said you could finish it tomorrow, why don't you come with me now?'*

Rosie kept her head down concentrating on her writing and the words she wanted to use. Through Rosie's lack of communication to Maria, Maria, turned and headed out of the classroom, out of the building, and ran towards the bus stop hoping to catch the next bus!

By the time Rosie had finished her writing, it was much later, and Rosie felt a pang of fear as she sat at her desk with her work in front of her. She looked at the empty desks without any students, desks with empty spaces and completely wrapped in silence. The eeriness of the silence made her move quickly. She took a second glance at the lightly green painted walls with the students' work displayed in different groups at different intervals. She had not seen the room look so empty. The coldness of the room made her shudder. She had not experienced this type of feeling before and knew that it was as other feelings; it was different and a little frightening!

She quickly packed up her books. Before leaving the room, she left her essay on the desk of the Mistress. She ran towards the bus stop where Maria had previously caught the bus home.

She looked at the timetable, and quickly glanced at the new watch she had been given by her sister for her birthday. It was now five minutes past three in the afternoon and much later than she had realised. The sun was hot on her skin; she knew the next bus would be about thirty minutes away. She thought, 'should she walk home or wait for the bus...?'

Rosie's mum was a graphic designer and worked mainly from home but today she was meeting a client at the office in Bologna. Rosie's dad also worked in Bologna and was a publisher. Rosie's sisters were both working, and one was studying at the University of Bologna and would sometimes come home for dinner but most evenings, Rosie and her brother would have dinner with their parents.

Rosie's brother is seven years older than her and is at Upper Secondary School (Scuola secondaria di secondo grado). His name is Ricardo. Rosie quickly gave a thought to Ricardo, 'Ricardo takes his lessons seriously and wants to study science when he's older!' She thinks to herself, 'He normally takes extra tuition after school, and I know he will be taken home by his tutor after five thirty this afternoon!' She quickly rules out a lift with Ricardo and his tutor.

Since Rosie was a small child, she had attended the Bologna Children's Book Fair and loved it. It was the family treat every year. Without exception, the family members would attend the fair at least once while it was on.

Rosie was still standing at the bus stop and thinking about the Book Fair as it was only a week away. As her father was in publishing, she would hear about the latest children's books at dinner tonight, she continued in her thoughts.

As she stood under the hot, clear, Italian, sun, she thought about her journey home and asked herself, 'what do I do now, do I walk or wait for the next bus?' She had decided to walk home.

It was an extremely hot and dry summer; the countryside was already turning to a light golden-brown colour. As she walked along the roadside verge, the dried grasses would crunch under her feet. At different times, Rosie took the opportunity to kick a sandy rock from her pathway, this made each step a little different and a bit of a challenge to see how far she had kicked the last stone ready to kick the next stone, and to see if it would go further!

She was deeply in her thoughts, thinking about the day, the book fair next week and the way she was feeling. A couple of weeks ago, one of her older sister's asked her to sit on a chair beside her and once sitting, the sister continued, 'you know Rosie, you are changing, and you will start to feel a bit different. You were once a child, but you will start to leave your childhood behind...!'

During the conversation, Rosie started to feel uncomfortable and felt she wanted to get up and run away from what her big sister was telling her, but she did not. Rosie had watched her sisters' change from girls to women, though realising they had changed, she took little notice of it!

As Rosie continued to walk, other thoughts came into her head. She thought of the older girl who had bullied a younger girl in the playground that day and was tempted to report it when she found out, that another girl had reported it!

She thought about the essay she had worked on until late and now realised, 'had she finished it tomorrow, she would have changed some of the words and phrases she had used...!' All these thoughts and more kept running around inside her head, and while thinking other new thoughts and ideas emerged!

With her head down, listening to the crunching of dried grass stumps as she stood on them and occasionally kicking a loose stone, she made her way up the hill, and in the distance, she could see her house! She knew from the fine column of smoke coming out of the chimney, 'that somebody had lit the kitchen boiler!' The fine whisps of pale grey smoke made their way into the hot, clear blue sky, of Bologna and beyond.

Chapter Two
Time Moves On

Early the next morning, Miss Rossi was in her classroom; she took the time out to read Rosie's essay before her class of students arrived. From her facial expression, she appeared to be satisfied with the girl's effort.

Some of the students did not eat breakfast at home, so the school provided the meal. Rosie had a group of friends that would always have their breakfast at school. Arriving at school, Rosie quickly saw her friends; she made her way to them. She had one special friend in the group, her name is Isabella. The girls met and instantly started talking about the book fair, now, less than a week away.

Isabella came from a big family of twelve children and was a middle child. Some of her older brothers and sisters were working in Bologna. One sister is training to be a florist and another works in a delicatessen, while another brother is training to be a butcher and another brother is training to become a chef.

Isabella, like Rosie, loved to work with words. Rosie had asked her father, *'please can you get Isabella a ticket for the book fair next week?'* As Rosie's father had a stand and displayed his books at the fair, he was given several extra, free tickets for his family and friends. Without hesitation, her father had agreed to Rosie's request.

Rosie was telling Isabella about the free ticket when the sound of the school bell suddenly rang out loud and clear. Departing, the girls agreed to meet up later in the day.

All the students were now back in their own classrooms. Rosie was now listening to Miss Rossi talking about the lesson plan for the day. Each child took down their notes as the Mistress spoke. Then Miss Rossi spoke of the essays that were written the previous day.

There are about 30 students in Rosie's class and each student's work was mentioned. Some of the students received good reports, while others were told by Miss Rossi, 'you know you have more ability than was written in your essay yesterday, please take the time to use the ability you have...!'

When Rosie's name was called out, Miss Rossi said, 'Rosie, I commend you for your essay, it was good, but you can do better...!'

With this announcement, Rosie felt her heart sink and was determined, next time, to try much harder.

The following lesson for the day was biology and this was not one of Rosie's favourite subjects, but with what Miss Rossi had said in the previous lesson, Rosie was now even more determined to try to make sense of the subject.

Biology, Rosie knows is the study of living things but that is as far as her interest goes! 'Everything else about biology is boring,' she thinks.

Her biology teacher was ready and waiting for his class to arrive; he knew that many of his students struggled with the topic, so he had decided to make the lesson a little different.

Rosie's friend Isabella joins this class for this lesson and the girls try to sit together if they can! Because the girls had previously misbehaved, the teacher had separated them. With different handouts and worksheets, this time, he had decided to see how attentive they would be before making them sit in different seats at different sides of the classroom!

As the girls met at the classroom door, they started to giggle and misbehave. Then, Isabella said something to Rosie that made Rosie stop in her tracks! The girls walked to the desks and seats, finding each a desk, and seat where they could sit together!

They both sat attentively as the lesson started and continued. The girls took down notes, made little drawings and worked extremely hard during the whole of the lesson.

The biology teacher was shocked by the work done by the girls. Never, before had he seen them work so hard. They were usually naughty, so disruptive, that he had to separate them to allow him to continue with his teaching of the lesson.

At the end of the lesson, the girls left the room as they had worked in the classroom; they did not play up or giggle as they had done in previous lessons.

The sun was again hot, and the day was dry without a cloud in the clear blue Italian sky. Rosie and Isabella were in deep conversation when Maria joined them. Maria wasn't at all interested in biology but loved sport and games; she wanted to be an athlete and would practise all different types of sports hoping one day to be an Olympian.

Little did Maria, at the time, realise that biology comes into every area of sport, and it would be a necessary subject for her too to study in the future...!

As lunch was not served at school, many of the children took a light meal or snack that could be eaten during their lesson changes. Some children took fruit and nuts while others took different breads, cheeses, and olives. Some children would swap their food for their friend's food!

Today, Rosie swapped some fruit with Maria for a piece of cheese. Rosie broke off a piece of cheese and together with some fruit gave it to Isabella. Isabella had brought some almond nuts and shared these with both Rosie and Maria.

The three girls found a place to sit out of the blazing morning sun to talk and share their food!

It wasn't long before the topic of the book fair came up. With this mention, Rosie nearly jumped out of her skin with excitement; she was now counting down the days and sleeps.

Just briefly, Rosie and Isabella mentioned the last biology class, but it was only a small mention.

Maria wanted to talk about the next sports day she was attending and how she was working hard in the gymnasium to keep her body flexible. The girls chatted for a while and then the school bell rang out and it was time to walk back into their classroom for the math lesson and later for the geology lesson.

Rosie was thinking about Isabella and what she had said before the biology lesson, this left her feeling a challenge and a feeling that she wanted to know more...!

The math and geology lesson went by, and Rosie was thinking more and more about Isabella's comments at the beginning of the biology lesson, now, two lessons ago...!

The last school bell of the day rang out, and Rosie, this time, was determined not to miss the bus home...!

Chapter Three
The Bologna Book Fair

The week had passed by, and it was the day of the fair. Rosie was to walk and meet Isabella at her house and then Rosie's dad would drive to Isabella's house to take the girls to the book fair.

It was early on Monday morning and Rosie walked over to Isabella's home to meet her. Isabella's house was always busy. Isabella's grandmother and an elderly aunty lived with Isabella and her family. The house was old and big with a great number of bedrooms and so many living rooms, it was easy to get lost if you didn't know your way around the house!

Isabella's father was a farmer and her mother stayed at home making different cheeses, picking olives when they were ready to harvest, and helping with collecting almonds ready to dry when they were also ready!

Sometimes, the elderly grandmother and aunty would also help with the harvest, make the cheeses, and do other jobs that needed to be done. Isabella's grandmother was known throughout the country area for her great food and when a festival took place, she would send Isabella's mum out of the kitchen, to be left alone, so that she could work and create wonderful recipes that led to great tasting food.

While this was going on, the elderly aunty would sit in the corner of the kitchen trying to give the grandmother information on what to do next with the recipe she was preparing. The grandmother would become annoyed at the interference by the aunty, then words in Italian, would be exchanged by the pair, and the aunty would sit in silence for a short time, and then she would say something extra that would further annoy the grandmother!

The kitchen at Isabella's house always had a food cooking smell coming from it. Because the house was so old, many generations of Isabella's family had been born and lived in the house throughout their lifetime.

Rosie stood waiting for her friend to come into the kitchen and looked at the activity that was taking place: saucepans of tomatoes were bubbling away ready to go into jars for storing. A pile of almonds in a great basket were sitting on an enormous kitchen table; these were ready to be cracked and the nut stored. Bunches of garlic were waiting to hang around the kitchen walls and lastly, and observing the kitchen activities, a tortoiseshell, coloured cat was sitting on a large stone windowsill.

Isabella came into the kitchen as Rosie's dad drove into the driveway. The two girls greeted each other and saying their 'goodbyes,' to the family, they then run to get into the car ready to go to the book fair.

On the way to the fair, Rosie asked Isabella about what she had said before the biology class the previous week. Isabella didn't have time to reply to her friend as they were now at the fair. The girls jumped out of the car at the crossing and made their way to the entry area where they were to wait for Rosie's dad while he parked the car.

The fair was already filling with people as Rosie's dad made his way through the crowd to meet up with the girls. He then said, 'Now girls, this is going to be a very busy day, make sure you always know where you can find each other. We'll walk to my stand and if either of you get lost, make your way back to my stand.'

Once locating her dad's stand, Rosie and Isabella made their way around the fair, they looked at books about fairies and fairy stories, books for babies and young children, musical books that played a tune when the pages were opened and turned, colouring-in books and many other interesting books. While Rosie was looking at a range of different, brightly coloured books, Isabella saw a stand with illustrated biology books. Rosie could not hold her friend back, she almost ran to the stand and closely behind, Rosie followed.

Isabella looked at the books, she went from one to another and to another. Some books were illustrated for very young readers, some for older children and some for Isabella and Rosie's age. Of course, there were books for university students, and some were very medical, but Isabella was interested in the books for her age.

Isabella looked at the books; all were open and before her on the stand! Rosie looked down at the open pages and when she looked back at her friend, she saw Isabella's excitement, she was so excited, she was almost at the stage of not being able to speak!

Isabella said to Rosie, 'This is what I want to do Rosie, I want to learn about biology and how living things grow and develop, I want to know more about this!'

Isabella asked the man managing the stand, 'Do you mind if I look through this book, I will just sit on the floor beside your stand if you wish?'

With Isabella's request, the man nodded his head, and Isabella sat down beside the stand and started to read!

Rosie could see her friend was deeply into the information within the book, with seeing this, she left her friend to find her dad's stand and to spend some time with him.

His stand was also very busy with great numbers of people asking questions about the story books he had published. Rosie knew a lot about these books as she had read a great number of them while her father wrote and produced some of the books.

Rosie found herself talking to adults and children about the new range of adventure stories her father's business had produced. Some of the books had 'pop-up' insides with the story coming into different dimensions, some were pirate stories and some books included farm stories for younger children.

The busy day was coming to an end and Rosie went to find her friend at the biology book stand; she was there, and she was still reading the books!

Rosie took a moment to stop and look at Isabella. Her friend sensed that she was being looked at; she looked up and gave Rosie a wave and then called, 'Come here Rosie, I want to show you something, it is very interesting'. With this, Rosie walked over to where her friend was sitting on the floor and joined her. They both sat, cross-legged, looking at the information and pictures in the book, that was resting in Isabella's lap. It was at this point, that Rosie too, took a deeper interest in biology!

Chapter Four
Friends Find A Common Interest

Rosie and Isabella walked back to Rosie's father's stand where they helped him to pack up the books and to tidy the stand ready for tomorrow!

The girls would be back at school tomorrow so they would not be able to attend the fair.

In the car drive home, both girls were feeling tired and did not speak much. However, Rosie's dad was speaking about the fair and how good the day had been – he was very excited about the reaction by people to his latest book list and did not stop talking all the way home!

Rosie's dad stopped the car first at Isabella's home where Isabella said, *'thank you for taking me to the book fair, it was a great day. See you at school tomorrow, Rosie,'* and then Rosie's dad drove back to his own home where Rosie's mum, sisters and brother were waiting to welcome them!

Rosie's dad was still excited about the book fair as he explained to the family, *'I've had an excellent day and have had some good orders come in for the new books!'*

He continued, *'...those illustrations you did for the children's pirate books Ann-Maria, are very popular and we have had good sales from them.'* He was making this announcement to Rosie's mum. Hearing this, a large smile came across her face as she served up the spaghetti onto the dinner plates!

Rosie ate some of her dinner but was too tired to eat any more food. She asked to be excused, left the dinner table, went upstairs to the bathroom, had a shower, cleaned her teeth, and went to bed.

Rosie slept a sound sleep in her softly painted, light-blue bedroom under the white, fluffy quilt. Before she knew it, her dad was knocking on the bedroom door, announcing: *'breakfast is ready, if you don't get up, you'll be late for the bus and late for school!'*

Hearing this, Rosie jumped out of bed, got dressed and ran down the hallway, down the stairs and sat at the breakfast table ready to eat her meal.

At Isabella's home, Isabella had woken early. She sat quietly on her bed and had been looking through her notes taken from the last biology lesson at school. She was trying to match the class information with the information she had learnt from the books she had read at the book fair yesterday!

She had thought a lot about the book fair and was hoping to go back to the fair before it finished. She thought to herself, '...with harvesting, both mum and dad are busy. Grandmother was interested in recipe books, and I doubt there would be any grown-up recipe books available at the fair.' She continued her thinking, 'aunty didn't seem to be interested in any form of book; I've not seen her ever look at a book...!' Then she thought of her younger brother and wondered, '...would he come to the fair with me?'

It was now seven-fifty in the morning and both girls met at the old, green, wrought-iron school gates. Isabella was still excited about the biology books she had seen at the book fair. She continued to tell Rosie about the information she had read and explained, 'Rosie, it was just so interesting... I could read that stuff all day long and not get bored!' Rosie listened to her friend as she told her more and more information about how living things had evolved!

The school bell rang, both girls made their way to their separate classrooms. Miss Rossi gave out the early morning information and the lesson plan for the day. Rosie and Isabella were to have their biology class first, followed by math, history, geology, exercise, and silent-reading time. Then, it was time to go home!

The bell rang out again and Rosie and Isabella met at the door of the classroom and were both ready for their biology lesson. They found their seats and were again sitting together. Both girls showed attention to their teacher as the teacher talked and gave demonstrations of how different cells worked within living things.

In previous lessons, their teacher had taught the class about how the heart beats, the lungs take in oxygen through breathing and how oxygen is needed to keep the brain healthy.

It was during the second half of the lesson, that Rosie started to take notice of what the teacher was saying. He was talking about 'change', just as her sister had spoken to her a few weeks ago...!

He, then said, '...to survive, living things have to change.' He continued, 'biology is a natural science that studies living things, in science we call these things, organisms. Biology science looks at the physical structure. If I can give you one example, an ant is different to a sheep or lamb, a spider is different to an elephant, a child is different to an adult, but these are all living things!

He repeats his information, 'The ant is different to the sheep, the spider is different to the elephant, and the child is different to the adult. We see by comparing these that their structure is different; they look different and are different. It takes chemicals to make these differences happen!

He continues, 'Molecules are a chemical and all living things are made of chemicals which are parts of compounds. Molecules are very exciting to learn about.

Not only do all living things have molecules, but they also have hormones. Molecules and hormones have a communication taking place. A molecule may talk to another molecule and a hormone may talk to another hormone. These conversations take place every day and every night while living things either rest or play. This conversation happens within the ant, sheep, spider, and elephant. In fact, there are millions of conversations happening every day and all night!

All people and children are made up of chemicals that help to form and are a part of each molecule and each part of each hormone. People and children also have lots of conversations happening within their molecule and hormone collection within their bodies, through the day and all night!'

Both Rosie and Isabella paid particular attention to the teacher and what he was saying about molecules and hormones. He then said, 'hormones have different personalities, some are happy some are sad, and they can create other feelings that we all feel!'

During the lesson, Rosie and Isabella had made many notes; they had taken down as much information as they could. After the lesson had finished, they had decided to meet up at Rosie's house to talk about molecules and hormones and how each person owned so many of them!

Chapter Five
Finding Hormones!

The next day, the girls had a busy day at school. Later that afternoon, Rosie and Isabella stood waiting at the bus stop; the sun was hot, they briefly spoke but both were excited.

In the distance, Isabella saw the orange and yellow bus coming along the road. The sun was beating down and the shimmer of heat waves could be seen, as the bus travelled along the hot and dusty route. The bus slowly stopped to let the girls get onto the vehicle. Once on, they showed their travel card and found a seat in the air-conditioned bus. Both sat down and both breathed a sigh of relief of the coolness of air the bus provides.

Rosie was the first to get off the bus. As she lifted her school bag to put across her shoulder, she looked down to her friend and said, 'see you in half an hour...!' Isabella nodded her head in reply. The next stop was Isabella's; she got off the bus and made her way along the lane to her house.

Isabella's mother had left freshly baked biscuits and freshly squeezed orange juice for her to have after school, both were on the large kitchen table. Her mother had left her a note, saying: '...in the fields, helping your dad with the harvest. Be home from Rosie's by five-thirty this afternoon, and ready for dinner'.

Isabella loved her mum's freshly baked biscuits; she ate them in a hurry and drank the orange juice to follow the biscuits down into her stomach.

She quickly made her way over to Rosie's house where Rosie was waiting in her bedroom. Both girls got their biology books out and sat cross-legged on the bedroom floor. Just as they were about to start, there was a 'meow' and a faint 'woof' at the door! Both Oscar and Felix wanted to join the girls as they went through their biology notes. Before the girls could start on their school revision, Rosie, got up from the floor to let the pets into the bedroom, had she not done this, the pair would have continued to demand their entrance into the room!

Isabella started to talk, she said, *'I didn't know that hormones and molecules communicated with each other. Our biology teacher made so many things clear for me today!'*

Rosie looked at her friend with interest, then replied, *'Yes, when Mr. Conti, said that; I could see why you have the interest in biology, it started to make sense to me also!'*

Just as the girls were talking, there was another knock on the bedroom door, and into the room came Rosie's mum, and one of her older sister's. Rosie jumped up to give her mum and sister a big kiss each. She was very happy to see them both.

Rosie's mum asked, *'What are you two girls so busy talking about?'* Then Rosie started to tell her mum and sister about the biology lesson they had today with Mr Conti. She said, 'mum, this is so interesting, I didn't know about this stuff until Isabella told me about it at the book fair yesterday!'

At that point, Rosie's older sister, who had trained to be a nurse, and was now at the University studying to be a doctor said, 'Yes, hormones are funny little things, they work inside our bodies all day long and some other hormones take over when we go to bed to sleep!'

Rosie's mum sat on the bed while she listened to the three excited girls talking about hormones.

'The first hormone that Mr. Conti spoke about this morning was a growth hormone,' said Isabella. She went through her notes and found a picture of the growth hormone.

Rosie's sister looked at the picture and laughed, she then said, 'That's the funniest hormone I've ever seen and I like the muscles on the arms...!' Rosie's sister then said, '...the correct name for the human growth hormone is somatotropin, but that word may be difficult to remember!'

Rosie looked at her sister and said, 'Mr Conti said, 'as we are all now over 8 years old, the hormones in our body will start to work harder, so we can expect changes.' Rosie's sister then said, 'Mr Conti is right, you will all start to change as you become young adults!'

She continues, '...girls change differently to boys!' Then Isabella quickly said, '...they have growth hormones also, but boys have different hormones to us..., that's what Mr. Conti said!'

Isabella continued to look through her notes as the conversation continued; she was eager to show Rosie's sister some of the other hormone pictures....

'Mr Conti said, estrogen is also a girls' hormone', said Rosie. Rosie's sister then replied, '...young girls and young women have something like estrogen, but it is called Estrodiol (E2). This is like estrogen, but this hormone is a little different when girls and women are younger...!'

She continues to talk, 'Estrodiol helps the young girl's body to mature into womanhood, when this happens, it is called *puberty.*' The girls' and Rosie's mum are interested in what Rosie's sister is saying, each look at one another, and nod their heads.

The girls are still sitting, cross-legged on the floor, while Rosie's mum sits comfortably on Rosie's bed, now wrapping herself in the white fluffy quilt.

Rosie's sister finished, she had her audience sitting before her and she wanted to share her knowledge and besides, she said to her mum, '*...this helps me to remember my notes before my exams next month*'. She continues, 'Women have

three major types of estrogen, estrone, estradiol and estriol which help the female body to grow and become ready for womanhood!'

Rosie's sister takes a moment to look at the faces of the hormones as they look back at her. They are there, displayed on Rosie's bedroom floor!

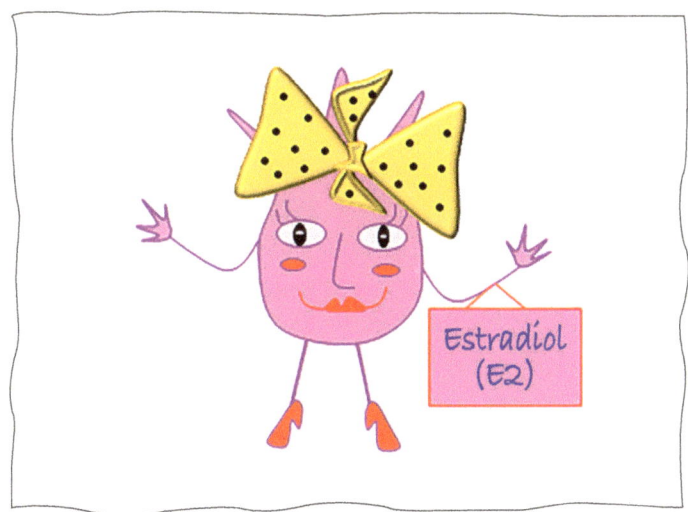

Rosie's older sister looks back at Mr Conti's images, she says, 'Ah, yes, now Estrogen is a more familiar hormone...!

As She now points her finger to the picture of *estrogen* and says, '*estrogen helps a girl's body to mature. It also helps to make her bones stronger and helps to keep her heart and brain healthy!*'

Rosie was astonished and asked, 'does it really do all of that?'

Then Isabella turned to Rosie and said, 'See Rosie, I told you this was interesting stuff...!' Rosie then nodded her head in agreement.

Rosie's sister now found the picture of ghrelin and laughed at the sad face that was looking back at her. Laughing, she says, 'this hormone has only recently been discovered!'

She takes a moment to think, and continues '...this is interesting science, this recently identified hormone, ghrelin, is the hormone that lets you know when you feel hungry!'

She continues, 'If you continue to eat once your stomach feels full and eat more than you need, this can become a habit. This is a complicated story, but if ghrelin is released when you are not hungry, then you may need to exercise, play sport, or do lots of activities to release the extra energy the extra food has given you. Some girls, as they enter puberty will naturally put on weight, this is the body's re-adjustment time from girlhood to womanhood!'

On hearing this, both girls wriggle a little, moving from side to side as they sit on their bottoms.

As Rosie's sister sees the next picture, she laughs out loud, and says, 'Yes, that is exactly what extra ghrelin does, it will make you eat "junk food" that is of no benefit to your body and if you sit and watch too much television, and don't do enough exercise, you will put on extra weight...!'

Another picture Mr. Conti had prepared for the lesson was a picture of progesterone. Rosie's sister laughed again at Mr Conti's drawing. Rosie's mum wanted to take a closer look at the drawing, when holding and inspecting it, she too, then laughed out loud and said, *'Goodness, that is a crazy hat that hormone is wearing...!'*

Rosie's older sister replied, *'as boys and girls grow, both girls and boys produce progesterone in their bodies. In girls, it helps to regulate the monthly menstrual cycle.' Like boys, girls also make testosterone!'*

Rosie's mum replied, *'testosterone...!'* *'Yes.'* replied Rosie's older sister. She then answered her mum, *'It helps to build a girl's muscles and is necessary for muscle strength...!'*

When the four had finished looking at Mr. Conti's drawings, Rosie's mum jumped up from the bed, and said, 'I can hear the car, your dad is home from the fair... I wonder if he's had a good day, and as good as yesterday?'

With the picture of testosterone uncrumpled, Rosie went on to look at the strange face looking back at her.

Breaking the silence, Rosie's sister, said, 'Have you got a picture of Gonadotropin[2], that is an interesting hormone?' Rosie looked at her sister shaking her head in reply, then replied, 'I think that is the one Mr Conti is going to talk about in our next lesson...!'

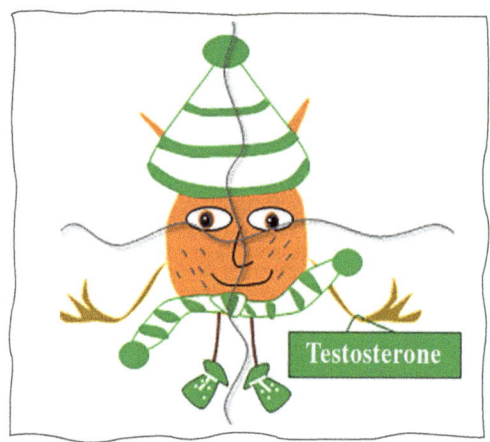

Rosie's mum, realising how late it was, gets up from the bed, goes downstairs and into the kitchen where the evening meal

---

[2] Gonadotropins regulate the growth, development, and function of the reproductive organs.

was simmering on the stove, even Rosie's mum thinks, 'how good it smells...!'

Isabella, realising it was now past five-thirty in the afternoon, quickly packed up her notes, left Rosie's home and ran as fast as she could up the hill and to her house where her grandmother and aunty were preparing their evening meal.

Her grandmother, said as she rushed from one job to another, *'it's nice to see you are here. Isabella, did you have a good talk with Rosie?'* Not waiting for her granddaughter to reply, she quickly returned to the large saucepan as the water started to boil over and onto the stove. Forgetting about her previously spoken question to Isabella, she quickly looked at Isabella, gave her a smile and said, *'...can you please set the table and help with the meal?'*

Chapter Six
Summer Holidays

It was close to the end of the school year and the summer holidays were only a few weeks away. Rosie and her family were going to Rome, where they would meet up with other members of the family.

Rosie was now preparing for her final school test and examinations which were happening next week. She knew she had worked hard in her biology and other lessons in the last term and was hoping for a good grade once the examinations were over.

She was excited about her holidays but had to stay focused on the tests and examinations and studying for them; once this was done, she could get ready for the holidays!

The tests and examinations were over, and the family was on holiday in Rome. Rosie was standing and watching the people at the Trevi Fountain but could not stop thinking about how the hormones inside her body were making her change.

She now knew that one day, she would start to look like her mum and her sisters. She thought about this, it was a little frightening for her at this time, but she now understood, 'how' and 'why' these changes were necessary. She had decided she would talk to her sister who was studying to become a doctor.

As she put the thought quickly to the back of her head, her cousins joined her and said, 'everything OK, are you coming with us to buy a gelato Rosie? We'll race you....!'

Part Two
WORKING TOGETHER
For kids and adults

KIDS' AND ADULTS' WORKSHEETS

Why do you need to have growth hormones working in your body?
....
....
....
....
....

Girls have estrogen, but do boys?
....
....
....
....
....
....

Estrone belongs to what hormone _ _ _ _ _ _ _ ?
....
....
....
....
....
....

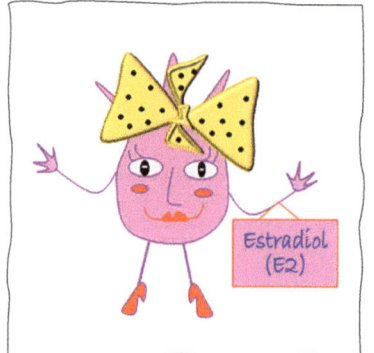

Estradiol belongs to what hormone _ _ _ _ _ _ _ ?
....
....
....
....
....

Estriol also belongs to _ _ _ _ _ _ _ and helps girls to go into womanhood
....
....
....
....
....

What is the benefit of having the hormone progesterone in your body?
....
....
....
....
....

Why do girls, generally, release smaller doses of testosterone?

....
....
....
....
....

All of the body's hormones play a role in keeping us healthy, what role does ghrelin play?

....
....
....
....
....

When you have more ghrelin in your body than your body needs, what does it make you do?

....
....
....
....
....

YOUR EXTRA NOTES

Part Three
WORKING TOGETHER
For kids and adults

LET'S MOVE ON

In the 21st Century, we need to take a realistic approach to our natural brain and body growth and the evolution we have gone through in the last four to seven million years. The myths and old attitudes, that limit healthy growth and wellbeing should now be left where they belong – in the past.

We now have technology that supports the science we can all work from. If for instance, it was previously thought the human brain was fully developed and mature at birth, this is now proven to be completely wrong. The human brain does not mature until a young person is in their mid-twenties.

From before birth, this unique tool needs to be protected until the young person can understand what they have inside their head. They need to understand its growth from the beginning to their age of maturity and into later life.

There is a lot to be said for the American guidelines: young people can legally drink when they are 21 years of age and not before. Alcohol can and is proven to damage the growing brain. This fact alone should put adults, all parents, grandparents, and carers on alert.

When an adult gives a young person, 'just a sip of wine!' or any alcohol of any kind, they are doing a great injustice to that person, and their future, and may cause irreversible brain damage; is a 'sip of alcohol' worth this?

As adults, whether you are a parent, grandparent or indeed do not have children of your own, we are all responsible, as a community, for the wellbeing of our young people. No one adult can avoid this responsibility.

It is time to take our heads out of the sand and to improve, right now, the future for our young people and the future generations.

We have seen, over the years, and more recently, shown by some young and older people, the lack of respect for other people, including females, people with differences and different customs within our communities; this is not only in Australia but continues to happen worldwide. This lack of respect has been and is being bred into national cultures.

Young people also need to understand respect and responsibility for their own body and brain, once this is done, it will reduce drug taking and the taking of other mind-altering substances.

Worldwide, the quality of the future will depend on the children being educated today.

YOUR GIRL CHILD

- From conception, girls are girls. Unlike boys, girls do not go through the chemical change and the development of the Y chromosome which allows the hormone testosterone to be produced. At eight weeks after conception, each boy child will start to produce testosterone in the cells of his body; this development encourages the growth of the penis and testicles. As with both boys and girls, when born, all parts of their bodies are in miniature.

  As previously mentioned, both boys and girls have testosterone in their bodies, but girls generally have less.

- When a baby girl is born, her vagina is only one to two centimetres in length. Like all parts of the human body, the genital area will grow in proportion to her natural size.

- At birth, a baby girl has about two million eggs in place within the ovaries which are attached to the fallopian tubes; these eggs are in-active at this time.

- A girl's body may start to change from the age of eight years, this change heralds the oncome of puberty. Once a girl goes into puberty, the female body, will release hormones that will allow the female body to grow and mature. This maturity shows firstly with breasts budding, pubic and body hair growth and menstruation will eventually take place.

- The menstrual cycle will usually start about two years after breast budding or between the ages of ten to twelve years. However, this is not always so. Menstruation can also start from the age of eight, though there does not appear to be a set time for this event.

What happens when a girl starts her period?

If a girl is not told about her periods, the first time can be daunting for her to experience. Over the course of twenty-one to thirty-five days; the usual number of days are variable but usually, about twenty-eight, the inner walls of the uterus start to thicken with extra blood. Over this time, a mature egg (ovum) is released from the ovary and travels down the fallopian tube. If the egg is not used to make a baby, it will travel into the uterus, the extra blood on the walls of the uterus will be released creating a period.

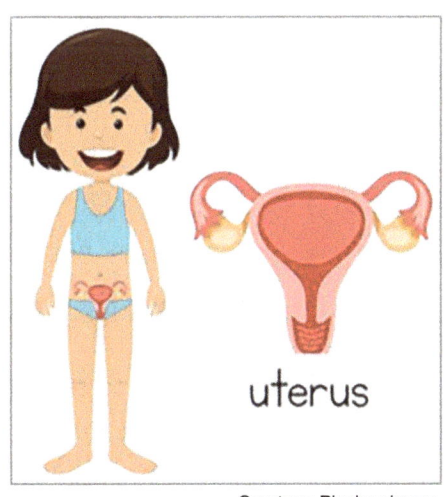

Courtesy, Pixabay image

The hormones that play their role in the female menstrual cycle

Are estrogen and progesterone.

 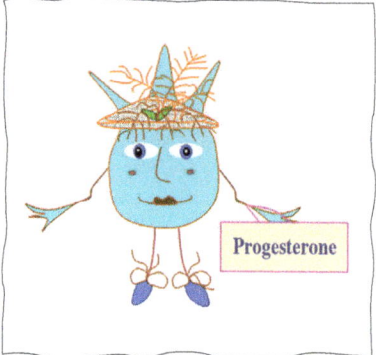

The stages of the period

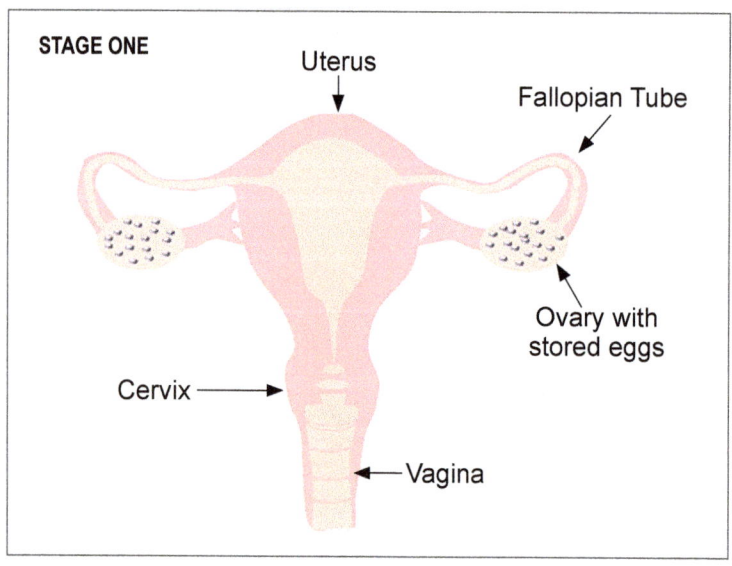

Before a period starts, the female eggs are stored in the ovaries, as shown in the opposite diagram. Through time and as she faces her eighth birthday, her body will start to change. The breasts may become tender, and she may experience a sore stomach or tummy, some headaches, and maybe, a sore or aching back.

Prior to the start of the periods, a mucus plug is released through the vagina opening. Our daughter's, if, we do not speak about this, may be alarmed when they see a creamy-coloured discharge when they go to the toilet, or it is seen in their underpants. This is perfectly normal and is the sign the female body is in good health and working properly.

It is at this point or within the next one to two years that the vagina will be getting ready to produce the first period for your daughter.

At about eight years, or before, speak to your daughter about her hygiene and explain about having in her school bag, a spare pair of underpants, a small sanitary pad, even a body deodorant is a good idea. The female body is changing, and many hormones and glands may start to work overtime while her body manages these changes taking place.

In the diagram below, you can see there is a thickening of the walls of the uterus prior to the beginning of the period. The mature egg from the ovaries is released and travels along the fallopian tube on its journey to the uterus.

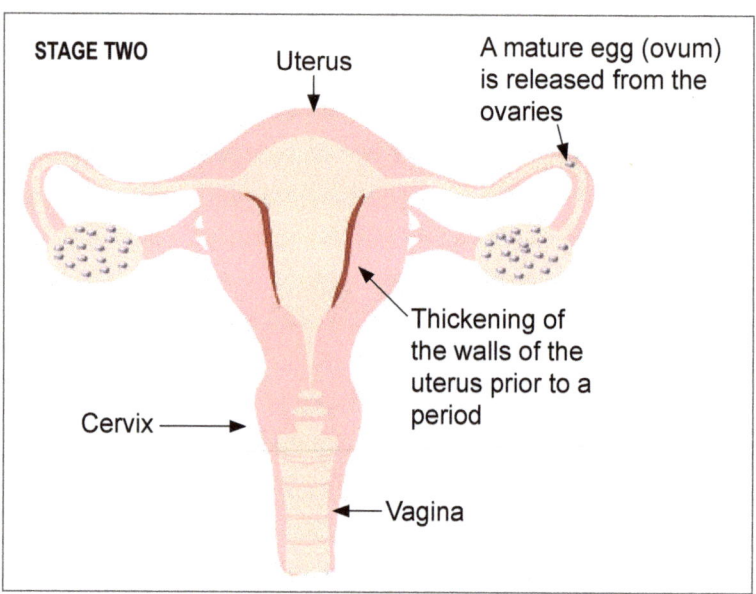

At this point, and if not made aware of how her body is changing, your daughter may feel or be irritable. However, if she is made aware of what is happening within her body, she will start to understand the reasons why she feels like she does!

In the diagram below, you can see how the wall of the uterus is thickening and the mature egg has moved forward and is about to enter the uterus.

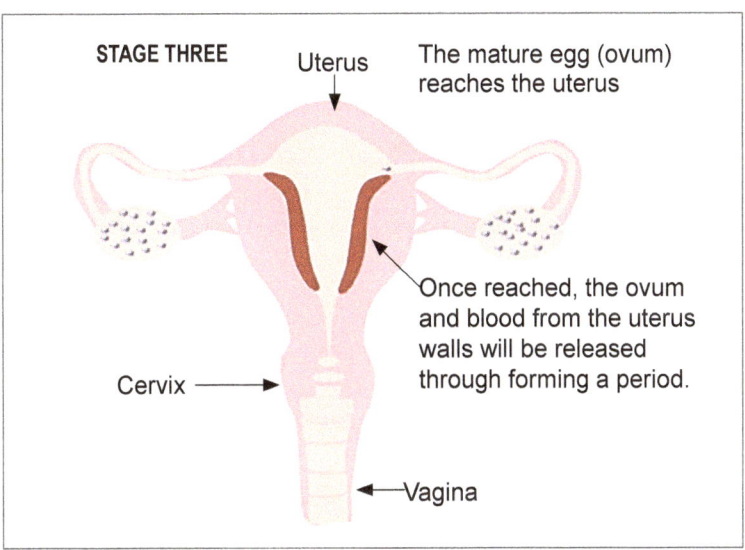

Each girl's cycle may be slightly different, so as you work with your daughter, do not become alarmed if her periods are at different times. Her body is also coping with the new demands that nature is imposing on her.

And finally, the day comes, when the period arrives. It should be a joyous occasion as our girls enter this new stage of life.

The first period can be light in colour and only last a short time. As I have said, all girls are different, and each girl's body will work to its own natural rhythm.

Once the period has finished, the cycle begins again. There is no mystery or intrigue to how the human body works in both males and females; the more openness to the subject, the less stress is placed on young people making the natural life journey into adulthood.

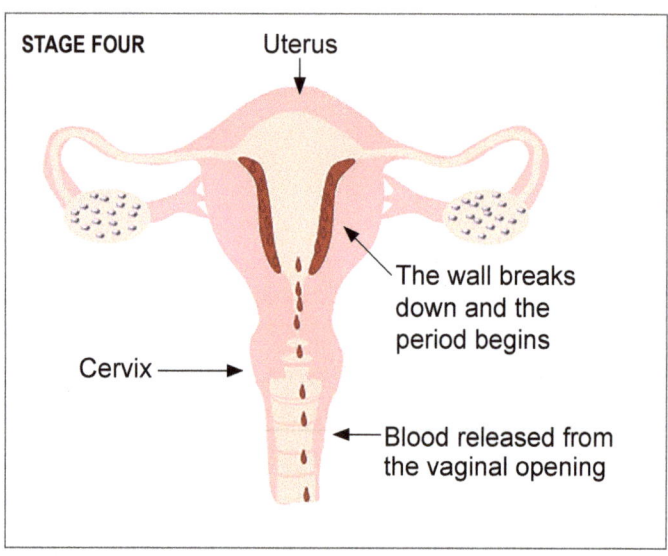

The female's body cycle and to repeat

Over the course of twenty-one to thirty-five days; the usual number of days are variable but usually, about twenty-eight, the inner walls of the uterus start to thicken with extra blood. Over this time, a mature egg (ovum) is released from the ovary and travels down the fallopian tube. If the egg is not used to make a baby, it will travel into the uterus, the extra blood on the walls of the uterus will be released creating a period.

The Female Menstrual Cycle

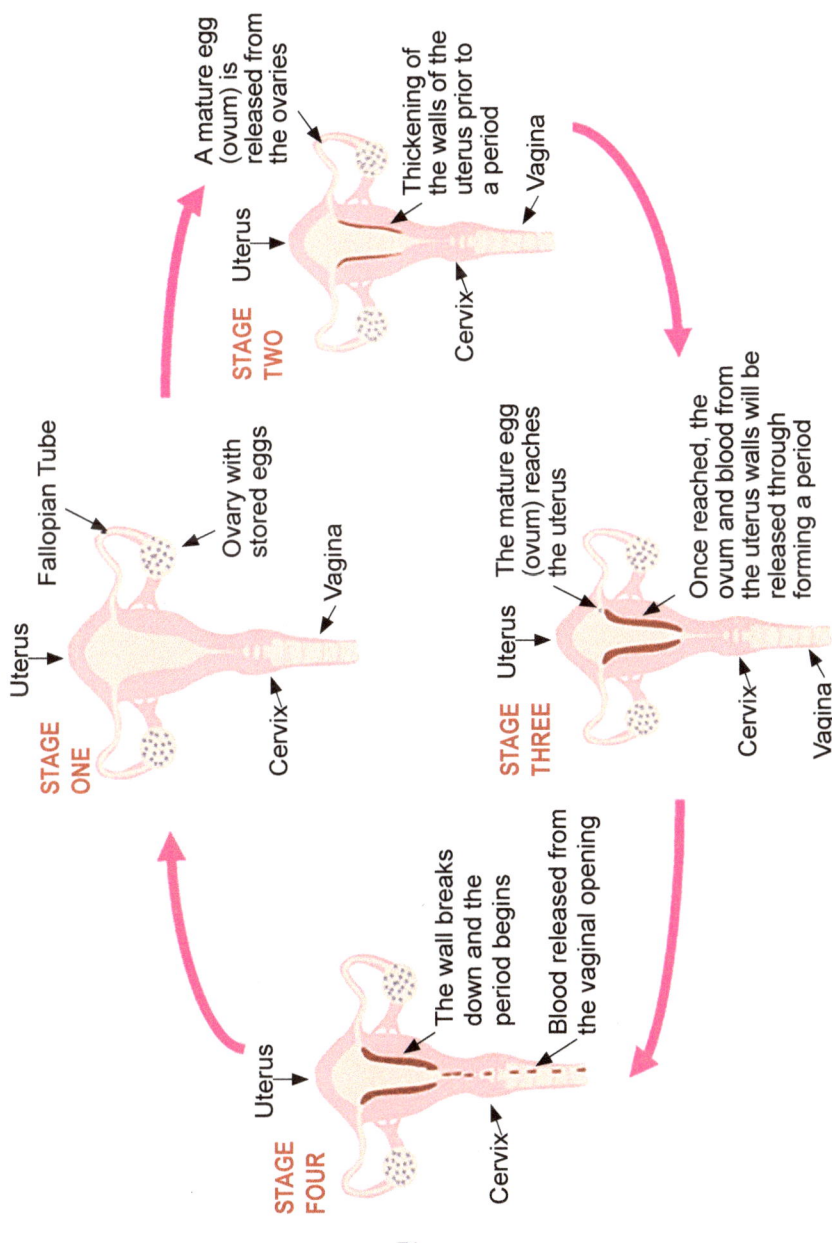

And then, the cycle then begins again!

This topic is further spoken of in the next book: Changes Facing Caitlin – Ages 11 – 14.

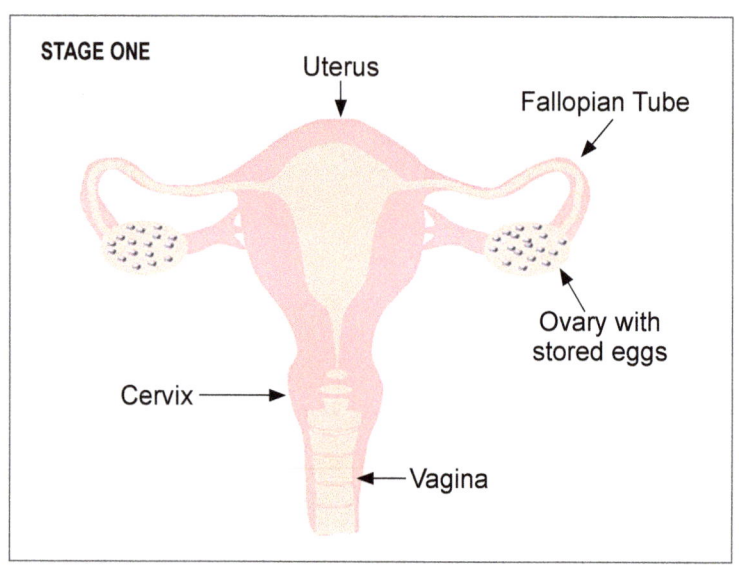

Your Notes

....
....
....
....
....
....
....
....
....

HORMONES - HOW? AND WHY?

Each of the four books identify how hormones play a major role in the changes we each experience, girls to women and boys to men, when going into puberty and growing up. In this instance, young females between the ages of nine to eleven years. This book is designed to make the journey of knowledge the young person gains, both enlightening and an enjoyable experience.

Throughout life, we each change differently. If a child is not made aware of its natural bodily and brain changes during these early years, changing from being a child to becoming an adult can be a frightening or difficult experience to think about or face.

Between the ages of eight to nine years, and some girls are younger when they start to notice change! During the time of change, a girl will start to experience changes in the way she thinks, sees the world, and feels. Her body shape will also start to change.

Hormones within a girl will trigger certain growth to happen within the female body. As previously mentioned, a girl's body will start with breast budding. This is a delicate time for some girls. During budding, the breast may become tender. Support can be given to girls by them wearing crop tops or light, supporting brassiere.

Some girls will put on a little weight at this time. It is important to encourage eating healthy food and to encourage playing some form of sport.

Some girls may start their periods at ten or as early as eight years, but periods can be delayed up until 16 years of age. Before a period begins, girls need to know about sanitary pads, menstrual cups, and period protection underwear.

ESTROGEN

Estrogen is the primary sex hormone in females. Women and girls have three types of hormones, estrogen, estrodiol and estriol. Estrogen binds together estrodiol and estriol during the reproductive menstrual cycle.

It is important for a girl, to not only understand her body, but to understand that change is a natural process and is a part of life's progression into adulthood. These changes are all brought about by the activation of hormones within the human body and brain.

When hormones start to do their job in young females, pubic hair will appear around the genital area and under the arms. It is to be remembered, that hair grows on the body and protects the skin from chafing and becoming sore. It also allows the sweat to run from the body which in turn, allows the body to keep cool during sport and other robust activity.

Hormones are chemical messengers that allow us to grow both physically and mentally. Without hormones doing their job, we would not be able to live our daily lives as we do. Hormones have always worked in our bodies and brains, and this has allowed the human species to develop into the people we are today.

Both boys and girls make the hormone estrogen in their bodies. Through my own research and teaching of up to forty years; teaching all age groups from children at primary school to university students and observing my own children and family members one thing has struck me; the number of headaches children have at the onset of puberty.

Research is now showing that low estrogen levels can contribute to light to severe headaches over this time of a child's development. There does need to be more research into this area, but we need to take more notice of a child if they say, *'I have a headache.'* If the headache persists, it makes sense to seek professional medical advice, but if a child says, please take notice.

A GIRL'S PROGRESSION STAGES

- **Stage One** – from zero to six or seven years. Girls can be more advanced in their development than boys at this age. Please do not worry, boys catch up. Girls will naturally learn, they love to be free, and will find fun playing in the garden; they like nature and will spend time creating their play.

    Girls, after the age of six months, girl babies will want more closeness to their mum or dad and don't often trust other people; this is a natural progression. Girls, at this age, show a natural connection to her parents, possibly more so her mother or female carer.

- **Stage Two** – from six or seven to about thirteen or fourteen years. Friends are important to girls. A bust up with a friend in the playground or during a game can be devastating to your girl. The corporate market has your daughter in their sights; they are continually developing their 'brand image' with your daughter's buying power, through your pocket, to buy! Learning through books is a great time filler and a healthy pastime.

- **Stage Three** – from thirteen or fourteen and into their mid-twenties, most girls will like boys. They also like to test their environment, your boundaries, try new ideas and new experiences. This can be a stressful time for parents and loved ones.

Like many suggested stages in the reality of life, there are differences. Each child is an individual person, will think, act, and learn differently. Each child will take on the world, do their learning and make their own decisions.

HOW KIDS LEARN - DEVELOPING LIFE SKILLS

As parents, carers, and educators, the boundaries we put into place for our children in the 21st Century should include the understanding of:

- ✓ **Free Will**
- ✓ **Reasoning**
- ✓ **Consciousness**
- ✓ **Respect**
- ✓ **Awareness**
- ✓ **Empathy**
- ✓ **Responsibility and**
- ✓ **Diligence**

From each of the above familiarities, please, consider the learning all children need to start gathering from the age of twelve months. Gathering such information should be within a child's everyday living environment, if it is not, it is not difficult to start to introduce each of the above ways of thinking. This can be done at story time or in everyday interaction with the child as it learns and grows.

A child's brain is always ready to undertake new learning, so let's take each of the above one at a time.

Free Will means that children are born with the freedom of choice. Children need to understand the difference between taking or making a good to a wrong choice; this is Free Will and is an essential life skill for adulthood.

Within **Reasoning** is the choice of Free Will. Children need to understand that within the choices they make, they are using their power of Reasoning.

Within Free Will and Reasoning there is a consciousness taking place in the thinking the child does.

When a child is young from the ages of six months to a year, there will only be fragments of these important life skills gathering and taking place.

Consciousness is an early learned skill by all children. Consciousness is part of a child's survival instinct and of stimulus and response. To give you some idea of this, a child knows when it is hungry and needs to be fed.

Respect is learnt and has guidelines within its meaning. Children will use their Free Will, Reasoning and Consciousness when understanding that Respect has guidelines, boundaries, and a sense of power within its meaning. Respect is a learned behaviour and carries with it the limitations that allow all people to live within their family, community and or chosen country.

Awareness is the behaviour that allows a child to evaluate, give consideration, and the knowledge that understands Free Will, Reasoning, Consciousness and Respect are to be woven into the thinking they do, their words said, or actions taken.

Empathy is the understanding that all people have feelings and each person's feelings should be respected.

Responsibility is the installing of the value that every action taken, or word spoken has an outcome and that each belongs to the child.

Diligence is a time of contemplation, commitment to the good of each: Free Will, Reasoning, Consciousness, Respect, Awareness, Empathy and Responsibility.

Life skills also include the adaption and willingness to learn new ideas, working hard and honestly to make situations work for both themselves, their families, and the wellbeing of their communities.

ESTABLISHING HEALTHY HABITS

Through learning, we have the ability, to teach our young people the qualities of life. This does not mean we teach them one way of thinking; it means we give them the mental tools to make their own right decisions. We do not take their learning from them – it means, we contribute to giving them quality learning through:

- Establishing respect for all people while working with workable guidelines.

- Establishing and taking the responsibility for the actions or words they say. If for instance you say, 'No' it should be taken for what it means, 'NO'. 'NO' is not a bad word; it is short, succinct and means what is said.

- Establishing regular meal and going to bed at a regular time each night only with minor exceptions to late nights.

- Establishing that screens and devices are only used after three years of age and for short thirty-minute daily intervals or less.

- Establishing from the age of five, the use and limited screen-time of one hour or less each day.

During a child's early development, it needs to flex its eyes to long and short distances, this builds eye muscle strength. Allowing a child to use a screen too soon, will contribute to weakening eye muscles and possibly future eye problems.

A child's pre-frontal cortex of the brain does not start to develop until six months after birth and takes a further five or six years to develop and eventually matures in their mid-twenties. Interference with the developing brain brought on through too much screen time, stress, cruel experiences or treatment, abuse, arguments, or threatening situations can interfere with young pre-frontal brain development.

- Establishing that a child needs to have creative and inventive play from its early development and before it starts to crawl.

- Establishing eating whole, good food habits from the time the child eats solid food. Whole good food does not have destructive, dead food additives added. Some food additives found in children's food may be derived from petroleum, coal tar, plastic, and other non-digestible substances, this can have a detrimental effect on the young and growing brain and result in other ill health problems either now or in the future. Remembering, that whole food drives positive healthy growth and productive learning.

- Establishing gross motor skills like using a broom, wiping dishes and other household chores.

Science is showing that children, boys, possibly more so than girls, when shown how to do simple household chores early on in their life, from about the age of four or five years, or earlier, they develop self-sustainability skills in caring for themselves later in life. Simple skill development in this way helps in brain development. Scientists aren't sure of why this happens; this research is ongoing.

A motto to learn to live with: 'Don't take the learning from the child.'

YOUR GIRL AND HER BRAIN

A girl's brain is different in the way it is constructed. It will double or treble in size in the first year of life.

To allow the brain of both boys and girls to grow, though the previously mentioned stages may be met at the suggested chronological age, the young brain takes longer to grow into maturity. When a young person reaches the age of about twenty-five, the brain is now working with all its architectural sections in place, and with the neuron pathways and connections firing as they should.

Neuron brain connections of both girls and boys continue to grow and mature; some will die and be replaced by new pathways, neurons, and their connections; this is especially so, when a child goes on to do extra learning either through learning a trade, academic studies, and other learning within sport, art, and other endeavours.

Change and growth are natural processes of the human body, brain, and mind. The human mind is always hungry for new information.

ACTIVE HORMONES, PERSONAL HYGIENE, WELLBEING, AND PUBERTY

Active Hormones

Hormones are activated through the central nervous system and sends out a message to the hypothalamus, 'CHANGE'. This release is Gonadotropin (GnRH) from the hypothalamus which is sent to activate the necessary hormones at the body's right time. When gonadotropin reaches the pituitary gland at the base of the brain, that produces two other hormones, follicle-stimulating hormone (FSH) and luteinizing hormone (LH). Once reaching puberty, these hormones are released in larger quantities.

The two hormones, follicle-stimulating hormone (FSH) and luteinizing hormone (LH) work differently in girls. These hormones give a signal to the ovaries to produce the female sex hormones, progesterone, and estrogen. These hormones are responsible for breast budding, (development of the female breast), and the womanly shape females have when compared to males.

Both females and males may go through a growth spurt during puberty. Like boys, girls may experience their hands and feet growing, and in some instances, their feet fit their mother's shoes, only to outgrow them in a few months!

About a year prior to the first menstrual cycle, a sticky cream plug will be released from the vagina; this usually means the first period is about a year away. The young female may also experience vaginal discharge which may be seen in underwear or pyjamas, or when wiping themselves after going to the bathroom. The release of vaginal fluids helps to keep the vagina clean and healthy.

Personal Hygiene
Sweat and oil producing glands can become active at the same time as puberty onset. This may produce clogged glands, resulting in pimple, acne, or skin breakouts. By washing their face twice a day; showering every day, especially after strenuous exercise or sport, and by wearing clean under clothes and keeping their body clean it will help to reduce pimples, and body odour. If a problem occurs and there are concerns, always speak to a dermatologist or health professional.

From the age of eight, females should be encouraged to have a small personal bag containing one pair of clean under pants, one or two sanitary pads; this personal bag sits discretely in the school bag. Doing this, will give our girl a sense of security should a period start at school. If it is needed, most schools carry sanitary wear. When visiting the school, bring the subject up with the teachers or head of the school.

Wellbeing

Most adults[3] walking on the planet earth have not missed out in going through puberty. Both boys and girls go through this stage of life, it is a natural life progression and is about reproduction and the continuation of humankind. It is to everybody's benefit that our young adults learn as much as possible about this stage.

Hormonal changes in both boys and girls can lead to emotional changes in behaviour. What was once a well-behaved child may appear to become a stroppy child that answers back, gives cheek and can, at times, be rude. There is no excuse for this behaviour and do not let the time slip, remind the child of who they are and what you expect of them, and one thing is not rudeness. Do not let a bad behaviour habit establish itself, if it is allowed, the behaviour patterns could follow into adulthood and cause more problem behaviour later in life.

Puberty

Puberty is about growing and 'Change'. It is about young people gaining their independence but gaining it so that it enhances their lives and does not lead to irresponsible actions or words.

Puberty is also about hair growth on the body, including arms, under arms, genital area, and legs. As puberty establishes itself, hair may become thicker, denser, or curly.

---

[3] Absent puberty is a condition that requires professional medical advice from qualified health professionals.

During this time, boys will add to their muscle density and mass, whereas girls may intensify in body fat. Both boys and girls should be made aware of the value and quality of the food they eat. Processed, and over processed food, leads to short and long-term health problems, science is now proving this.

ROLE MODEL AND MENTORS

The role of quality role models and mentors in your child's life cannot the emphasised enough.

During all stages of a child's development, both boys and girls, it is important to include within both their family and friend contacts positive role models.

As previously said, only include those people you can trust with your child which may include, grandparents, aunties, uncles, older cousins, or trusted friends. Such people will give your child a positive person to speak to when they have concerns; this may not be you. Do not be alarmed if it is not you. When a child seeks other trusted adults to speak to, it is a healthy sign that the child is growing and will want eventually to be in control of their own life.

Different people come from a different perspective in life and will possibly take each situation differently, and without emotion and may work to a different level. Such role models allow your child to build positive self-esteem, build independent points of view and are always a 'safe place' in times of stress or conflict.

UNDERSTANDING HOW THE HUMAN BODY GROWS AND MATURES & RELATIONSHIPS

'Changes' Meeting the National Curriculums of Australia and the United Kingdom

HORMONES WITH HATS

CURRICULUM OBJECTIVES – AUSTRALIA

Incorporating and supporting Year 4 to 6, ages 9-11 years. Personal, Social and Community Health (ACPPS070 – ACPS076 - ACPPS071 - ACPPS072 - ACPPS073 – and other related areas of the Curriculum including:COS3.3, DMS3.2, INS3.3, TLF-IDM021182 Scootle.edu.au).

MEETING CURRICULUM OBJECTIVES – UNITED KINGDOM (UK)

Natural body changes for girls between School Years 4 to 6, ages 9 to 11 years.

(Health and Wellbeing, Relationships, and Living in the Wider World)

Relationships Education, Relationships and Sex Education (RSE) and Health Education.

'Effective RSE does not encourage early sexual experimentation. It should teach young people to understand human sexuality and to respect themselves and others. It enables young people to mature, build their confidence and self-esteem and understand the reasons for delaying sexual activity. Effective RSE also supports people, throughout life, to develop safe, fulfilling, and healthy sexual relationships, at the appropriate time.'[4]

---

[4] Relationships and Sex Education (RSE) (Secondary) - GOV.UK (www.gov.uk) Extracted from 'statutory guidance Relationships Education, Relationships and Sex Education (RSE) and Health Education & Australia: https://www.scootle.edu.au

ONLINE SCHOOL PACKAGES

Full Potential Training offers a range of education packages, with our school packages for 'CHANGES', Children Growing Up, we cover the sensitive area of puberty and the changes that naturally occur in males and females. The story book at the beginning of each book allows the child to become familiar with the role that hormones play in making these body changes happen.

For young males with the ages of nine to eleven years, we have developed, 'CHANGES' Facing Kian. The girls' book is 'Changes' Facing Rosie. The books have been developed with discretion and to allow the child to quietly absorb the story board about the changes they are either going through or about to go through. We cover many sensitive areas of the subject of puberty, and how the female and male body works as the change occurs.

We offer a complete online package, which includes the story book. The online education packages do include the changes that both males and females go through during the time of puberty. They are not directed to one sex but both males and females. Once ordered, the package is downloaded from our server to the school, college, or holiday programme at your location.

The Package for Changes, Females and Males, Children between the ages of 9-11, children have one by two hours sessions, and children between the ages. 11-14 has four by one-hour sessions, including a continuous 'voice over' with each slide. There are pause times for discussion and some question-and-answer sequences.

We ask that courses be ordered at least two (2) months in advance, this allows us to print and deliver the children's books to your location and in time for the lessons.

Please keep in mind, all children are different and learn differently, the information on how the human body changes as children grow and mature, may vary from home to home and each person's perception of growing up can be different. Our books and courses are well researched with only up-to-date information included in the contents of the books and education programmes.

The package meets both the Australian and United Kingdom objectives within Social Community Health and Relationship and Sex Education.

For more information, please email,

admin@fullpotentialtraining.com.au
Or, see our website, www.fullpotentialtraining.com.au

FAMILY PACKAGES

For many people, discussing puberty and the 'Changes' that take place within the human body are private discussions. They may not be easy discussions to have, but it is a necessary part of a parent's responsibility to their child or children.

For those people, we have developed Family Packages that include one book and a CD that is the same as the School Package.

If this allows you to discuss this topic with your family in private, please contact, admin@fullpotentialtraining.com.au

Or, see our website, www.fullpotentialtraining.com.au

Thank you for reading 'Changes' facing Rosie,

For the follow-up book,

Please see Changes Facing Caitlin

11-14-year-old girls

Published by How2Books

www.ingramcontent.com/pod-product-compliance
Lightning Source LLC
Chambersburg PA
CBHW062042290426
44109CB00026B/2706